Of Love and Wine

by:

Jer-Bug *and* Bobby Cenoura

Of Love and Wine

This is a work of fiction.
Names, characters, places, and incidents either are the product of the
author's imagination or are used fictitiously. Any resemblance to actual persons,
living or dead, events, or locales is entirely coincidental.

First paperback edition September 2024

ISBN (paperback): 979-8-3304-4032-0

Cover design/Artwork: Christian Mirra
Layout design/Text Illustrations: Bobby Cenoura
Editor: Teri Edwards

Published by Slice of Pain Publishing and Media, all rights reserved.

Other works published by Slice of Pain, Publishing and Media LLC:
Dating Up: They Hypergamy Factor; Male Angst Vol. II: Smokin' Thuy'd (Part 1 & 2);
Male Angst Vol. I: FML: I Always Get 'Those' Chicks;
Black Names Matter: The Black Names Book.

All the aforementioned titles can be found on multiple platforms
such as Amazon, Apple Books, Nook and others.

*Jer-Bug's dedicates this to his
loving wife of 44 years;
Bobby dedicates this to
John and Katherine Reynolds,
two monumental and instrumental
people that helped him to
heal and grow.*

CONTENTS

Of Love and Wine

by:

Jer-Bug *and* Bobby Cenoura

SPOTTED LANTERNFLY

𝒮LIFFIES

(Spotted Lantern Flies)
October 30, 2023

Once in a peaceful small vineyard,
Its watchful winemaker came ajar.
A bug from the east, settled down to a feast.
Tranquility came unleashed and so marred.

This pretty red spotted creature
Sought to unleash a plague feature.
In droves, they came, not caring of blame.
See the lighting-fast little eat-ures.

Destine to settle in well,
Fly in the wind, and then fell.
Grape vines, they sought, unaware
they'd be fought,
Ringing Mr. Vineyard-Man's bell.

Oh, what a gut punch they hatched,
Mating spring kiddies to unlatch!
Their coming brought fear, trembling.
Oh dear!
Flooding, they'd come in a batch.

Up from his heels, he sprang,
Spraying nasty Sevin on the gang.
They thought they were well.
Destruction would fail.
Oh, the alarm had been rang!

On, the guy would not stop.
Shooting spray cans up rows, he would pop.
He poisoned these fiends, saving
spring scenes.
Field cleared, each little guy got a bop.

Diligently searching for egg sacks.
Expectation—then scraping off their racks.
In a bag, they would come and go, county
dump for a stow.
Fall harvest saved from these quacks.

Red-Eye snapper, swept-back thing.
Tri-angle bug, spotted-wing.
Season end. Can't defend.
Flip away, crushed to stay, Madam Ming.

So there, the battle is done.
Let these losers ruin our fun?
These flickers from China—don't let
these guys bind ya.
Toss these guys. Drink our wine. War won.

℘OETRY

January 17, 2011

Poetry as Arts provides not only
Life's "how?" but Life's "why?"
Poetry is like the wind; it frees its reader's
imagination and lets it soar.
Poets see chaos from the clouds.
Poetry is simple elegance.
A poet shows his people itself through
the mirror of Truth.
A poet is a craftsman—not of chisel
and stone, but of word and thought.

Emotion is the soul of poetry, with
rhythm and rhyme its pulse and
heartbeat.

Inspiration is seldom transferable, for it is
a gift to the soul of the poet.

When my Creator touches me on my
head, tears come out.
Poetry cuts, washes, and allows a heart
to heal.
Along with my watch, I keep all my
poems in my vest pocket.
A gold chain links us together.

Abandon a verse, abandon a child . . .

Love a radical poet.

Treble Goddess

September 28, 2014

Shimmer silk in blanket darkness,
Velvet tones seek grief to lose.
They siren tales of the heartless.
A love's exile sings the blues.

Glimmer rays flood the show girl.
Her life's amuck, so seeking lull.
Painted face framed by the lock curls,
Glares radiate from angelic dull.

Minstrel Mannequin, sing the blues.

Voice melodies of selfishness.
Screech soprano of shattered heart.
Shielded tears yield their distress.
Senses sweat, stressed, then depart.

Glow, image of surreal sorrow.
Bellow forth these tortured days.
Grasp your dreams, though they are
borrowed.
Wail, promote a staggered way.

Ceramic Chagrin, sing your blues.

Pour out your being of forced concessions,
As Blank and Empties emit their stares.
Shout forth crystal soul's confessions.
She's open, tender—yet, life's not there.

Treble Goddess lives her blues.

ᴛHE ᴘARKING ꜱPACE

February 25, 2011

I love you and I search for you,
licit beauty of mine.
The sun, moon, and the stars—so
dim to your shine.

I search the mountains, valley floors,
the plains, and the forest.
Don't hide from me. You've heard
my cries, oh my lovely lurest.

You own my heart and soul, you do.
To you I will be true.
Again, you hide. Oh, love of mine,
let me fondle you.

Your slender shape and waiting arms fill
me with intoxication.
Yet, you run and hide and bring in guys
for my provocation.

With tears and beers, I come to you, your
loving arms are waiting.
You tear my heart and wrench my soul.
Suitors, you are baiting.

Come with me. Yes, you, my dear.
Oh, thing of style and grace—
When we're one, its heaven's fun,
oh charming parking space.

Night's to fall and I must go.
Leave you space, I must.
Our sun goes down and darkness falls
on my tears and lust.

The morning comes, I search again.
Oh, Diamond, "The Sought After."
A suitor's there and in my place.
Woe to me, disaster!

Green Pea Soup

March 3, 2014

At breaking dawn, the house is dark
with no guiding light for me.
Asleep in bed as I embark, rests
the slender form of Lee.

Sleep my fair of many springs,
radiant as the morn.
Create a home and hearth for kings,
amuse with buck and fawn.

I'll breakfast on her green pea soup, find
a lawn filled deep with snow.

Feed animals and secure the coop, and
skirt the storm a foe.

White bellies perch on our dogwood tree,
fluffing the wind and chill.
Sunshine brings a chance to dance about
the grass of dill.

Find your joy, it's at your feet—you'll
leave your life and times.
Contentment's there, just look and
seek—life's just a verse of rhyme.

cDRAGON cALONG

July 26, 2010

Mary's little friend, Gravier, had a garden she held so dear.
Kept her veg's in little rows—a site to see, everyone knows.
"Grand patch here!" her sign displayed.
"Tomatoes, cukes are sweet today!"

Over flew a dragon of fun,
With a tail that glowed with the setting sun.

"Oh, land here, please, oh, charming gent!
You'll please us all, if you're so bent."

With such grandeur, he settled down.
Stories and smiles he passed around.
Without a thought, he started to dance.
Too garden close, he mauled some plants.

Two steps then, SMUTCH, for he had dozed—

Gravy would scold with eyes that froze.
"You knocked some veg's again, I see.
I told you last, your tail's not free."

Shocked, surprised, he had been warned.
Still, Gravy made him so forlorn.
Lifting wing, he gently left, smiled, and waved—he'd lost his jest.

"Come back soon, our dragon love.
We'll wait for you with kisses and hugs."

"I'll try my best. I love you so . . .
But my tail follows me wherever I go!"

MON TUES WED THUR FRI SAT SUN
03 04 05 06 07 08
10 11 12 13 14 15 16
17 18 19 20 21 22 23
24 25 26 27 28 29 30

Calendar Cowboy

November 30, 2011

Calendar Cowboy of sleek body frame,
Can a love compete with your beauty
and fame?
See your lasso and saddle, blanket
and bridle—
Can you love me forever, have a face
that says, "I will?"
Pin-up Cowboy, whom ladies adore,
Will you forsake the herd, love me
evermore?

Bare-breasted Cowboy, with a look
far-away,
Can you be gentle and tender, keep
life's wolves at bay?
In buckles and cowhide, so chiseled and tall,
Will you shop and walk with me in
the malls?
Saddled Herd Rider, are you all
about show?
Are you hollow and empty—all glitter,
no glow?

High mountain Cowboy, with a body
of brass,
Can you love and cherish, make a bond
that will last?
In your western outfit, you look so
appealing.
Can you cope with my world of emotions
and feelings?
Spur-booted Ranch Hand, see some
ladies swoon…
For me, will you rope and lasso the moon?

Calendar Cowboy, steady as a rock,
Are you patient through mood swings?
If so, I'll take stock.
Will you wipe snotty noses, love me with
the flu,
Be devoted and attentive when the
mortgage is due?
Pin-up Cowboy, are you selfless or vain?
Will I find me a Cowboy and make a
home on the range?

CRYSTAL LADIES

May 5, 2011

City Lady of Glass and Stone,
how is your heart?
Could you make me a home?
Demand and control in a boardroom,
you can.
Mind, I'd give my heart to a Raggedy Ann.
You're sleek and cool in crushed
wool's embrace.
You're a lady of what—glitter or grace?
Strut through my streets, my vision of love.
Attractive and smart—have you come
from above?
Self-contained city girl, how is your heart?
Is it open to another? Will you do your part?

City Lady of Steel and Brick,
Have you a heart of love, or mischief
and tricks?
Climb that ladder, you strain as you spiral.
Will you listen to me, give credence
to my will?
Your arm's hooked on Prada.
Wow, that sway as you walk!
My glasses fog up with your chattering talk.
The angels envy your heavenly face,
Though courtship is more than a
smiling embrace.
Self-contained city girl, you've a
life to unfurl.
May I catch your attention?
May I give you a whirl?

Marble Lady of Quick-footed Pace,
Is there a heart under that satin and lace?
Have you left your family for the
"Apple" alone?
Is your emotional safety net just your
cell phone?

Studded high-heels with long-leg appeal,
Will you consider my needs?
On my will, can you yield?
Is there life within you?
Have you a heart to share?
Can you suffer for me?
Are you willing to care?
Self-contained city girl, do you live
all alone?
My heart, if I give it, is not to be thrown.

City Lady, Jasmine Lady, with a step
that invites,
Will you let someone in, past that
"air" that will bite?
Chin up, eyes down, city lady on
city streets,
Rattled and shaken—I'll make a
chance that we meet.
Feathered hat, matching scarf—
how you accessorize!
Have you a heart of slate?
Are you playing disguise?
Hearts, though not made to be broken,
should be given away,
To one so deserving, to one here to stay.
Self-contained city girl, you're as
sharp as a brick.
In this City of Glamour, don't get
cut on the glitz.

City Ladies of Broadway in Towers of Stone,
Show me your heart! Show me your soul!
Are you warm to the touch, or
city-street cold?
Self-contained city girl, finding love
takes a toll.
Are you, MY ONE, to have and to hold?

JAZZ
BAR
p
f

JAZZMAN

April 19, 2012

Play for me, oh Jazzman!
My love has left me cold.
My soul aches from her lies
and deceptions bold.

Wail away, oh horn man!
Blast me with your shrills.
Drive away my teardrops and
these unfaithful chills.

Scream at me, oh Jazzman!
Blare out your melodies.
Her hollow heart discarded me—
my broken heart's now free.

Blow, tenor man, blow away!
Dissipate my pain.

Your music comforts shattered hearts.
I have loved in vain.

Blues me down, oh Jazzman!
Cast off decadence.
Search for me, a love so true of
mystic flowery scents.

Whisper trifles, velvet man, as cool as
a summer's mist.
Seek for me a beauty—one yearning
to be kissed.

Murmur sleek groans, Jazzman.
You'll find me all alone.
Your sounds reach deep inside of me,
sounds of your saxophone.

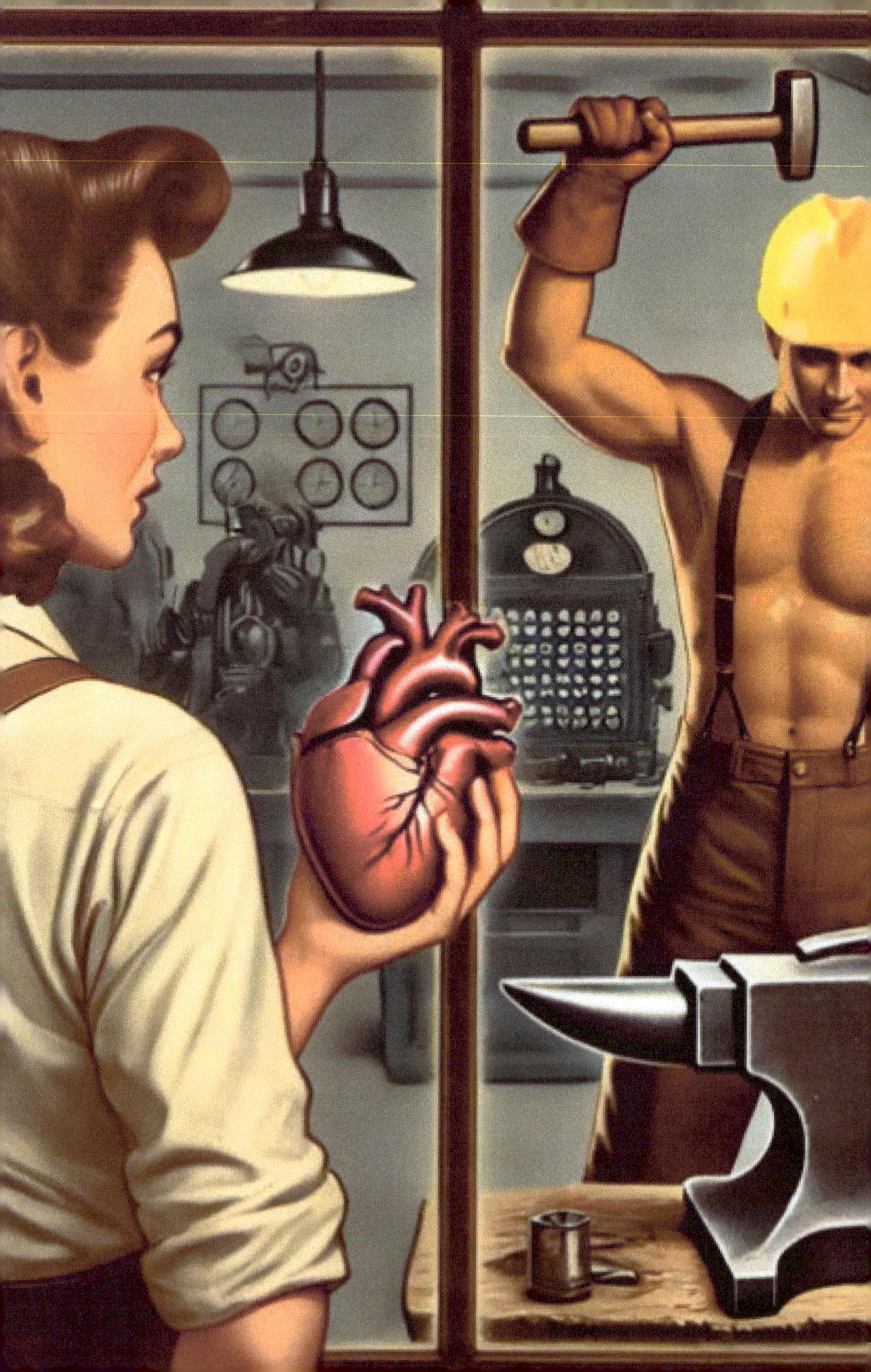

My Iron Man

June 26, 2011

My iron man turns bolts of steel,
Supporting us, he will not yield.

I love his grease-stained hands
and arms.
He speaks of work, yet, for us he longs.

My iron man has a face of leather.
Though his back will ache—our child,
he'll get her.

My iron man has feet of clay.
He concrete stands on them all day.

He has massive shoulders and a
silver mind.
Kids come to him—he's gentle and kind.

My iron man has a heart of gold.
He talks to garden birds, I'm told.

"Go now, night-shift! Hands of brass."
We'll kiss at dawn. This too will pass.

I see him strain as the years set in.
He works with engines. Our life, he wins.

Home from work, to his chair he'll rest,
Then fall asleep. He'll get my best.

My iron man turns bolts of steel.
His love for us, he will not yield.

I love him with my heart and soul.
I care for him as we grow old.

Soul Maiden

December 14, 2014

Trek Rica maiden, through tropical greens,
Seek a paradise among east island scenes.

Quick-paced spindle-legs, fly up
coral steps.
Envy moss-ed falls your sleek
sparkling pep.

Rendezvous empty heart, present
serenity to him.
Accompany your soul beach in its
sun-setting dim.

Court oneness with suitor of bronze
chest and abs.
He offers abundance of shrimp,
clams, and crabs.

Footprint turtle cape track little flippers.
Acquaint the Caribbean under stars of
the dipper.

Nestle on a marine throne.
Search eyes, find a kiss.
Tomorrow's poor solace.
Too soon gone . . . hurting. . . and. . .missed.

Toy Box Tempest

June 15, 2020

Cindy Carburetor of satin and lace,
Flowing mass of locks surround.
Roving eye for Ken abounds.
Gold disc earrings led fall from grace.

Sought from toy box among the crowd,
Unrivaled desire among the dolls.
Seek, taunt, wit of Gauls,
Arrayed in silk, beyond proud.

"Lure my love away from me!"
Barbie and Ken, couple one.
Made from ages, sun to sun.
Discard to toy bag. Go! Flee!

Battle dolls. Jealousy sought.
Rise anger. Provocation sown.
Ripped from hand—yanked, thrown.
Desiring tempest, behavior fought.

Strewn to floor, crashing down.
Child sends foot to Cindy's chin.
Stripped from waist for roving sin.
Yanked from play—recycled, drowned.

Disgraced, discarded as broken toy
By Mom and child of years five.
Torn, rent. See stress abide.
She shredded parties, picnics, joy.

Despaired to Abyss's timeless bounds.
Capture Ken, Barbie's pal?
Ken is Barbie's soulmate. POW!
Incisive, dastardly, heartless, foul.

Disgraced doll. Banished. Gone.
Innocence lost. Shunted fawn.

$\mathcal{A}$BOUT THE $\mathcal{A}$UTHOR

Jerry Scuderi, known affectionately as Jer-Bug, combines his meticulous writing approach with his winemaking prowess to craft poetry that resonates deeply with life's experiences. With a mind attuned to linguistic puzzles, Jerry's poetry reflects his methodical yet creative process, where each word is chosen with care to evoke the essence of his subjects. His unique talent in winemaking, particularly in producing award-winning estate wines, mirrors the precision and passion he brings to his poetry. In a recent collaboration, Jerry has partnered with Bobby Cenoura, a literary visionary, to create illustrations that beautifully capture the feelings and emotions conveyed in his poetry, making their work a harmonious blend of art and verse that invites readers into a richly textured world of sensory and emotional depth.